T0354589

A HISTORY LESSON
PRECEDING
THE 2012 ELECTION

A HISTORY LESSON PRECEDING THE 2012 ELECTION

Gene Cordes

authorHOUSE®

AuthorHouse™
1663 Liberty Drive
Bloomington, IN 47403
www.authorhouse.com
Phone: 1-800-839-8640

© 2012 by Gene Cordes. All rights reserved.

No part of this book may be reproduced, stored in a retrieval system, or transmitted by any means without the written permission of the author.

Published by AuthorHouse   07/19/2012

ISBN: 978-1-4772-2140-2 (sc)
ISBN: 978-1-4772-2141-9 (e)

Any people depicted in stock imagery provided by Thinkstock are models, and such images are being used for illustrative purposes only.
Certain stock imagery © Thinkstock.

This book is printed on acid-free paper.

Because of the dynamic nature of the Internet, any web addresses or links contained in this book may have changed since publication and may no longer be valid. The views expressed in this work are solely those of the author and do not necessarily reflect the views of the publisher, and the publisher hereby disclaims any responsibility for them.

This book is dedicated to my wife of sixty-four years, a former Lady Marine, who almost singlehandedly raised our three children due to my extensive travels as a Federal Auditor.

INTRODUCTION

The first section of the Introduction will be devoted to the younger generation of Blacks, Whites, Yellows or Browns to give them something to look forward to in their lifetime.

I have to start with my experience as a nineteen-year-old Helmsman, one of three on a Navy Reefer (6,000 tons without radar equipment to tell our position) when I was wakened about 4 A.M. from my bunk from the sound of general quarters. I grabbed my life jacket and went to my gun station. I waited there until the Sun came up on October 12, 1945, and we sighted trees for the first time since leaving the Battle of Okinawa on September 12, 1945. We traveled 6,489 miles from Okinawa at a speed of about 11 knots, experiencing a typhoon in the China Sea and the only ship to survive the worst typhoon on record.

We were shipwrecked on Nootka Island, off of Vancoover Island, for twelve days with holes in the engine room from the rock formation. We hit at high tide, and we could walk off the bow at low tide. A Canadian salvage tug wrapped a 5-inch steel line around the superstructure and pulled us off at high tide after twelve days with pumps at work until they took us up the Juan de Fuca Strait to Seattle and drydock for repairs.

I had a 30-day pass on Christmas Eve and hopped a train since no airline was available. I arrived in Chicago on Christmas Day and found an airline available at 6 P.M. I arrived in Washington, D.C. and caught a cab that took me home at 10 P.M. When I arrived, my Mother advised me that my girl friend, a former Lady Marine, was home next door. I told her that I would "check that out the next day" for the happiest day of my life.

By the way, I have had no regrets for volunteering to join the U.S. Navy with a "home wherever I traveled". I also took advantage of the "G.I. Bill" and attended night school for five years—a privilege still available, as I understand it, for veterans.

The second section of the Introduction will also be devoted to the younger generation. After marrying my former Lady Marine on September 20,

1947, and attending night school for five years, my wife and I sought to buy a house, but the mortgage lenders would not recognize her income, probably because she might have a baby (and rightly so). I then sought to buy a lot and build a house on it myself. I found a reasonably priced lot in the countryside and purchased it. Incidentally, there were several people doing the same thing in the countryside. So, I got acquainted with one of them, and it paid off. He told me to purchase a book entitled "Your Dream Home" by Hubbard Cobb and Sigman-Ward (Illustrators & Architectural Consultants). Copyright 1950, Wm. H. Wise & Co., Inc., New York. Price around 1954, $6.50.

The book contained 560 pages with many illustrations; seven different home plans covering 145 pages; and 32 pages of Glossary to understand building terms. A worthwhile investment. I built the home, with my wife's help, for half the price of a small house with two bedrooms on the open market. It was a real challenge with no regrets, and I was about 30 years old when it was finished with most of the work on weekends and using my vacation time. One final note: check with your local Health official before completing your lot purchase for any problems with a well and septic system with a drain field.

Thus, I have spoken for the younger generation to give them hope for the future as I had hope after surviving my ordeal in WW II and took advantage of the "G.I. Bill" for my education; and met the challenge to build my first house with the help of my wife that I was proud of as a Former Lady Marine who gave birth to our three offsprings (that have developed into their own success stories).

One final thought for the younger generation. Albert Einstein was one of the greatest scientists of all time. He was quoted as saying "Imagination is more important than education". Nevertheless, a minimum of two years of college is a good "calling card".

The third section of the Introduction will describe how I became a first generation American in 1926 with my Mother arriving with my Grandmother from France in 1903; and my Father arriving from Germany all alone in 1903, having been requested by his Aunt and Uncle to work in their bakery which turned out to be one of the largest in Washington, D.C. My Father was 18 years old during the voyage, and had he been 18 in Germany, he would not have been permitted to leave because the ruler of Germany was saving manpower to serve in World War I. My parents bought a town house in 1921, six blocks from the Nation's Capitol. This section will also describe my wife's background as a third generation American with Irish and English background, and later in life volunteering for the Lady Marines in 1944 and one of only 19,000 Lady marines who did not serve overseas, but relieved a Marine to fight overseas. My military service will also be summarized. I will continue to highlight the important events of my lifetime covering 85 years including the challenges as a Federal Auditor, and interesting aspects since retiring in 1985 and publishing three books since that time.

* * * The author wishes to acknowledge the source of data in Part VII—THE BIG SLIDE from the book entitled "LOSING BIN LADEN" by Richard Miniter. Copyright 2003. Reprinted by permission of Regnery Publishing, Inc., 1 Mass. Ave. NW, Washington, D.C. 20001.

TABLE OF CONTENTS

THE EARLY YEARS

I had a step-sister born in 1913 whose Mother died shortly after birth. My Father re-married in 1915 to my Mother who was born in France and she raised my step-sister as if she were her own. My brother was born in 1919 and a sister in 1925. I was the last to arrive in 1926. My Father was very fortunate in 1929 since he worked in a bakery owned by his uncle and never suffered from the depression. Likewise, my wife-to-be's Father was a railroader for 50 years and never suffered from the depression. During that trying time, he picked up coal spilled from gondolas to fill bushel baskets for neighbor's coal furnaces. Likewise, my Father brought home bags of bread from his uncle's bakery for neighborhood families.

My brother, Joseph, finished high school in 1937 and sought jobs for a year before becoming a stock clerk for a department store at two dollars a day for a six-day week. Times were tough and unemployment was 17% in 1937.

I followed my brother into high school at St. John's College High School and was taught by the Christian Brothers. I worked after school and on saturdays to help pay the tuition. There was no tuition for grade school taught by the School Sisters of Notre Dame at St. Joseph's Church and School. Both schools rendered an excellent education. When I graduated from High School in 1944, there was an early graduation in February for those reaching 18 years of age and subject to the draft.

I volunteered for the Navy in the spring of 1944 to avoid an Army draft and never regretted it. When I finished "boot" training and had 30 days leave, I was surprised to learn when reaching home that a classmate who graduated in February and had been dating my sister, Elizabeth, had been killed in the "D-day" offensive in Europe. A second classmate, in a class of 72, was later killed in Europe. A third classmate was wounded by a grenade at Iwo Jima causing him to lose his right leg. He suffered for many years, and former Marine, Willian Logan, Jr., died in 2010. The first death in 1944, who dated my sister, was Robert Rill; and the later death was Thomas Hanrahan.

GROWING UP FAST

When I returned from my 30 day leave pass, I was surprised to learn that I was one of three sailors assigned to ships. The balance of the 120-man company were assigned to the Amphibious forces primarily for landings in the Pacific. I was ordered to Miami for "sub-chaser" school covering a variety of subjects including ship & airplane recognition (friend & foe), familiarity with depth charges, and going to sea on a "Sub-chaser".

When my 6,000 ton cargo ship was completed by the Beaumont, Texas, shipyard, it was commissioned on April 3, 1945 at Galveston, Texas, with an 80 man crew consisting of eight officers and seventy-two enlisted men.

After a 3-day shakedown cruise, we set sail for the Panama Canal and, eventually, Pearl Harbor. As one of three Helmsmen, I had a "ring-side" position from the "flying bridge" when on duty.

It was a spectacular position when going through the many "locks" of the canal; and more spectacular when entering Pearl Harbor and witnessing the many ships anchored there that could spare no time for "chipping & painting" in many instances. In comparison, our new ship, recently completed, was shining brightly.

After loading two refrigerated holds, one frozen and one chilled; and a third forward hold primarily for potatoes, the U.S.S. ATHANASIA (AF41) left Pearl Harbor on May 29, 1945. Drills of every type were held daily while underway. Gunnery exercises with towed sleeves for targets were held upon leaving Pearl Harbor and upon arrival in the Marshalls. Eventually reached Ulithi in the Western Carolines where we picked up a convoy with picket vessels for protection. On the night of June 25, 1945, our last night before reaching Okinawa, we remained at general quarters from 11 P.M. until 3 A.M. The anti-aircraft firing of our picket vessels was so effective that no enemy planes reached our convoy. We provisioned 68 ships in Kerama Retto, Okinawa, while protected by smoke from launches at night.

We provisioned forty ships at Hagushi Bay, Okinawa, after leaving Kerama Retto. Getting the ship ready for sea, we remained at Hagushi until July 12th, awaiting a Ulithi convoy slow enough for our speed.

Returning via Ulithi, we arrived in Pearl Harbor on August 4, 1945, completing a 10,000 mile cruise which kept us at sea for forty three days, excluding a 3 day stop-over at Ulithi. The usual rush of loading took place at Pearl Harbor, and we departed on August 8, 1945. Issues totaling 374 tons were made to 23 ships at Ulithi. On August 29, 1945, we sailed in convoy for Buckner Bay, Okinawa, arriving there on September 4th. During the following six days, 1220 tons of provisions were issued to 57 ships. 71,000 pounds of potatoes and 21,000 pounds of onions were surveyed due to excessive temperatures in the forward hold. While at Buckner Bay, we witnessed a kamikaze attack on an ammunition dump on the shore.

During our return trip, we were caught in a typhoon which we found terrific in the China Sea, and at one point, took a 45-degree roll since we were travelling light without cargo to weight us down for the propeller (since the Captain would not take sea water to make up for the absence of cargo). On

September 29, 1945, we received news that we had been diverted from Pearl Harbor to Seattle, as a result of the Japanese surrender (President Truman's decision avoided an invasion of Japan). Without radar equipment to tell our position, and the Navigator unable to shoot our position due to cloud cover, we were shipwrecked in Canada as described in the Introduction. After my 30-day pass, I reported to a Receiving Station in Washington, D.C. and ordered to the west coast where I boarded a 27,000 ton Aircraft Carrier, the U.S.S. HANCOCK (CV19) with a crew of 22,000 men. When I left in June of 1946, completing two years of service, and starting as an Apprentice Seaman, I ended as a Second Class Petty Officer with a commendation that stated "The loss of this man's services to the U.S. Navy is to be regretted."

GETTING TO KNOW MY NEXT DOOR NEIGHBOR

When I was 16 years of age, my sister asked me if I wanted to go to a dance in Southern Maryland. I said "Sure". She and her husband, and our "adopted brother", and myself took off for a Saturday night dance. Our adopted brother said to me as we entered the dance hall "Gene, that looks like the girl that lives next door to you on Capitol Hill. Why don't you ask her to dance?" I replied "I think I will". So I approached her table and asked her to dance. As I found later, she was with two cousins and one said to her "Why don't you, Helen?". So we danced and I found that she was visiting two cousins in Southern Maryland who had a farm with a country store and a bar room. I later found that she lost her Mother due to medical malpractice in 1935, before antibiotics were available, and lived with her Father. This was 1942, so I saw her occasionally until the Spring of

1944 when she volunteered for the Lady Marines and after "boot" training, was assigned to Camp Miramar air base in California. I later found that her Father was a sailor in WW I; her brother was a Navy Chief Petty Officer; her uncle was a Navy Chief Petty Officer with Amphibious warfare; another Uncle was an Army Medical Officer with the rank of Major; and his son was a Navy Medical Officer who ascended to the rank of Admiral and held the position of Deputy Surgeon General of the Navy. So, when she volunteered for the Lady Marines in the Spring of 1944, I volunteered a short time later for the U.S. Navy. The rest is history when I returned on leave and learned from my Mother on Christmas Day, 1945, that she was discharged and at home next door as described in my Introduction. Also, I failed to mention that she was third generation Irish and English, but Irish was shining all over her.

THE SURPRISE OF 1951

I sought a gastroenterologist on Connecticut Avenue in Washington, D.C. in 1951 concerning an ulcer. After the examination, I entered his office to hear the results and recommendations. I must interject that Dr. Matthew Perry was a distinguished medical professional, and after reporting on my condition, he relaxed and anxiously described one of his patients years ago who suffered the worst case of ulcers he had ever seen. The patient was Secretary of State Cordell Hull in the FDR administration. He resigned due to poor health in 1944, and died in 1955 at the age of 84. Dr. Perry proceeded to tell me that President Roosevelt sent two henchmen to his office while Secretary Hull was still part of his cabinet, and asked for Secretary Hull's medical records because the President felt that he should be retired. Dr. Perry responded in his usual distinguished manner and said "I told the SOBs to get the hell out of my office". He then proceeded to tell me that Secretary Hull was the only honest man in Roosevelt's cabinet, and that was the reason for his severe case of ulcers. That is not the end of the story. About two years later, I was watching an interview with a retired reporter on one of the network channels. He related being called into Secretary Hull's office somewhat before the Japenese attack on Pearl Harbor. He went on to say that Hull told him that the people in Hawaii had to be warned of the impending attack by the Japanese. The reporter then asked if the President was aware of the impending attack and Hull's answer was that the President was aware of it, but the people must be warned. The retired reported then displayed a copy of the Honolulu newspaper dated about a week before the attack, and it read "Japs to attack Pearl Harbor". History proves that no one paid any attention to the headline.

An earlier rumor that the Japenese code had been broken was proved correct, but the warning was delayed to provide a surprise attack to unite the country to fight. The bloodpath occurred with 3,681 deaths and/or wounded and eighteen ships were sunk including the Arizona with half of her crew entombed in the ship. Fortunately, three carriers were on maneuvers and absent from Pearl Harbor. Therefore, their availability was a God-send. Now we know the true nature of FDR!

MY PUBLIC
ACCOUNTING CAREER

I was employed by three public accounting firms before entering Federal service. One of them was the Alexander Grant & Co. with Maury Stans, CPA, as a partner in the firm. While in their employ, I worked under a contract with the Postal Service. When Maury Stans began his Federal career and eventually became a part of President Nixon's cabinet, I naturally was interested in following his career. At one point, he made a profound statement as follows:

> "In government finance, there is no acceptable alternative to conservatism. Anything else is speculation, and that means gambling—with the nation's security, its strength, its future. History shows that economic soundness alone

doesn't guarantee a nation's greatness,
but no nation has ever been great
without it."

How true and more applicable today with the Obama administration. President Obama has placed our great nation on a fast track for financial doom. His huge spending has not improved the economy, but merely added to our National Debt that our grandchildren will still be paying interest on. Only one objective can explain his actions: To grow the Federal government as he has thus far with an addition of 159,000 Federal jobs, and to enslave our nation in communism with Obama as the dictator! We must elect a Republican President this November to reverse this trend!

I was also employed by the Henry S. Owens CPA firm on Connective Ave. in D.C. Mr. Owens knew that I was a WWII veteran so one day he advised me that he was approached during the war to take a Federal job. He responded by saying "I know nothing about the Federal government, so I would be of no help". It is true that it is a different "ball game". But Mr. Owens was one of the first CPAs dating to around 1937. He also had the best of clients in the Washington area primarily performing audits as opposed to "keeping books".

This brings to mind when President Reagan took office in 1981 and searched for government savings. A staff employee of a leading CPA firm came to work at the Office of Management & Budget (OMB) for two years selling a new concept and then returning to his CPA firm to "rake in the bucks" as did other firms that took over the auditing of billions in government spending. This work would supposedly free up Federal auditors to search for "fraud, waste and abuse" savings. This never happened. The CPA firms did not report large findings so as to obtain repeat engagements. As an example, one of the last Federal audits questioned $62 million dollars in a six-month period whereas the CPA firms over the years report an average of $2 million in questioned costs for a six-month period. Nevertheless, if larger amounts were to be questioned and they held up, the entity audited would fill the void with other projects on their waiting list. The Federal auditors should be returned to these audits of billions in government spending and at a much lower cost then charged by CPA firms. Incidentally, the CPA firms celebrated this takeover with a convention of 4,000 in San Antonio, Texas that lasted four days. The convention was described by the L.A. Times from June 10 thru 12, in 1984.

MY FEDERAL
AUDITING CAREER

My Federal Auditing career started in 1956 at the National Security Administration; thence to the Federal Power Commission; the Army Audit Agency; the Naval Audit Office; the Naval Propellant Plant at Indian Head, Md.; the Federal Aviation Agency; and finally, in 1970, the Department of Transportation that changed into the Office of Inspector General for the Dept. of Transportation in 1980. Thence to retirement on December 31, 1985.

The most interesting aspect while at the Federal Aviation Agency in 1963 was my loan to the Flight Standards Service for four months for a study of Aircraft Maintenance Bases authorized by the FAA Administrator, N.E. Halaby. The study entitled "Project Pre-Flight" resulted in a 160 page report reflecting millions of dollars saved in Aircraft

Maintenance Bases and Presidential Citations signed by Lyndon B. Johnson and Administrator Halaby on January 15, 1965 for all seven members involved: Robert L. Sicard, Chairman; Kurt H. Schilling; George S. Fox; John R. Cranage; Francis J. Taylor; Richard G. Brown; and Eugene R. Cordes (Auditor).

There were other interesting aspects of my exposure to the Office of Inspector General for the Dept. of Transportation, but too numerous to describe in this document.

THE BIG SLIDE

The Big Slide began around 1995 and is best described by Richard Miniter's book entitled "Losing bin Laden: How Bill Clinton's Failures unleashed Global Terror" in which he describes the number of missed opportunities he had to capture and imprison or kill the terrorist leader Osama bin Laden, but instead, we are still hunting him after the four-plane hijacking/destruction on 9/11/01. In one instance in 1996, Sudan's Minister of State offered to arrest and turn over bin Laden and asked "Where should we send him?", but a CIA official stated "We have nothing we can hold him on." The author points out that the Clinton foreign policy was to get re-elected, and therefore, anything that might be controversial had to be avoided. The reader is reminded that, if Clinton had accepted one of these offers, the slaughter on 9/11/01 could have been avoided, and our military deaths and injuries overseas would not have been necessary as an aftermath.

In addition, Attorney General John Ashcroft testified before the September 11 Commission in 2004 that the Clinton administration's FBI technology budget through September 30, 2001 was actually $36 million less than the last bush budget eight years before, thus hampering tracking of terrorists, and also taking aim at one of the September 11 Commissioners for creating a "wall" in 1995 between law enforcement and intelligence gathering which would have been vital before taking a step toward sending a large military force overseas to Iraq and/or Afghanistan.

Moreover, columnist Oliver North described Clinton's defense of pre-9/11 actions during a Fox interview in September 2006 as violations of three Executive Orders in 1976, 1978 and 1981 barring political assassinations. Clinton stated in that interview "I worked hard to try to kill him (Osama bin Laden). I authorized a finding for the CIA to kill him. We contracted with people to kill him. I got closer to killing him than anybody has gotten since."

Last but not least, President Clinton had a scandalous relationship with a young White House intern, Monica Lewinsky, whom he charged with lying, but her soiled dress proved otherwise.

My research for several days in an Annapolis law library has shown that the greatest blame for our deep recession/near depression lies with President Clinton's signing of a 1999 Public Law 106-102 that repealed Sections 20 and 32 of the Banking Act of 1933 (12 USC 377 & 78) designed to prevent another Great Depression. While President Clinton signed the law containing 143 pages, and the repeal consisted of two sentences, three Republicans sponsored the bill and share some of the blame for the two sentences, i.e., Senator Gramm of Texas, Rep. Leach of Iowa, and Rep. Bliley of Virginia, all of which are no longer in public service on Capitol Hill. Of course, Clinton could have been upset over the Lewinsky affair and had no interest in what he was signing.

The repeal negated financial penalties for coordinating mortgages beyond the bank or financial institution first handling the transaction. This paved the way for useless mortgages to travel to foreign countries in Europe and eventually contribute to their financial woes. The basic problem from the start of these mortgages was the lack of checks for the ability to make periodic payments for the mortgages. The beginning of the end had commenced.

Hindsight is always better than foresight, but the senior Bush proved his caution in the 3-day incursion into Iraq with a sigh of relief when it was over. Not so with the younger Bush after visiting the destruction of the twin towers. I might digress with my Carrier Hancock's Chaplain, James Doyle, who incidentally gave up his helmet to many dying sailors while under fire, and so impressed the ship's photographer that he said of him "The first man I had ever known who had completely conquered fear". At our ship's reunion in 1994, he surprised many of us by saying "I'm all for Clinton invading Haiti" (a trouble spot at the time). He added "As long as Clinton leads the troops ashore."

How true. Perhaps President Bush would have thought twice before ordering our military into Iraq if he had to lead them ashore. You may recall that there were many roadside bombs that caused deaths, injuries, and I suspect, many of the suicides that occurred.

Nevertheless, the younger Bush showed anxiety to retaliate for all of the destruction of 9/11/01. I am sure that he was unaware of the impact of a lesser budget for FBI technology and the creation of a wall between law enforcement and intelligence gathering, both of which were essential to an overseas deployment. Moreover, Richard Miniter's book revealed, for the first time, how Clinton and a Democratic Senator stopped the CIA from hiring Arabic translaters with phone intercepts from bin Laden remaining untranslated.

Storm clouds were gathering for the younger Bush. No only did he, as Commander-in-Chief, send a large military force overseas without the benefit of intelligence gathering, but it was not long after, that the financial crisis was felt with sales of thousands of homes facing foreclosure because of two sentences repealed in a 1933 Banking Act, designed to prevent another Great Depression, that President Clinton signed into law in 1999 with three Republicans sponsoring the 143 page law, but Clinton takes full responsibility by signing the law! The full impact of this law permitting home sales without credit checks appeared to climax in 2009, and a ripple effect throughout our economy has ensued ever since.

Of course, President Obama played the "blame game" during his campaign and ever since taking office, blaming President Bush for everything imaginable, even after President Obama has been in office since January 20, 2009, over three years ago. The economy has suffered greatly, the job shortage is unbelievable, the unemployment figures do not include all those who stopped looking for jobs, and President Obama's trillion-plus budgets has increased our National Debt from ten to fifteen trillion and still growing. Also, fuel cost is beyond reason, thus adding to the cost of food, but President Obama still precludes drilling on land or nearby waters.

What do we know of President Obama's background? The Washington Times published syndicated columnist Tony Blankle's (recently deceased) "Media chronicles—Obama remains unknown" on September 24, 2008, prior to the November election. The article described how the mainstream media had gone over the line and were now straight out propagandists for the Obama campaign. "Balanced" reporting by the major newspapers throughout the country, except the Washington Times, no longer existed. As a matter of fact, former Democratic Senator from Georgia, Zell Miller, attended the Republican convention in 2000 and stated "This is not the Democratic party I remember in the past." How true.

In addition, we do not know what to expect in the upcoming election in November of 2012 when Attorney General Eric H. Holder released a Black Panther with a weapon in his hand at a voting station in the 2008 election and stated "We do not prosecute blacks for intimidating whites". What has this country come to with the Obama administration?

VOTER FRAUD THREATENS UPCOMING ELECTION

On November 1, 2008, World magazine carried a story entitled "Stock the vote—registration shenanigans in several states prompt investigation of ACORN", article written by Jamie Dean. ACORN stands for Association of Community Organizations for Reforn Now, and they claimed that more than 13,000 workers in 21 states signed up some 1.3 million voters. In Ohio. Freddie Johnson, 19, says he filled out 72 voter registration cards for ACORN. Officials are investigating ACORN's voter registration in at least eight states.

The U.S. House of Representatives' Committee on Oversight and Government Reform issued a Staff Report on April 1, 2010 entitled "ACORN Political Machine Tries to Reinvent Itself". It identified the rebranding in 13 states by various names. Moreover, the Washington Times published a story on June 20, 2011 by Robert Knight entitled "Vote fraud becoming rampant" in which he described Florida election officials finding in 2009 that at least 888 phony voter registrations submitted by ACORN officials with arrest warrants issued for 11 ACORN employees. In 2009, a Cleveland ACORN employee was caught re-registering the same person 77 times. Voter fraud investigations targeting ACORN were launched in 12 states.

Voter fraud threatens the upcoming election in November, 2012! The "Tea Party" organization had a demonstration some time ago that involved thousands gathered at the west side of the Nation's Capitol and stretching nearly to the Washington Monument. The majority of the news media played down the numbers because they fitted the aforementioned article by Tony Blankle that described them as "straight out propagandists for the Obama campaign". One reporter questioned one young man in the huge crowd who informed him that he slept in his car for two nights in order to join the Tea Party crowd—a sign that many people felt it was important to show up in the Nation's Capitol to reflect their displeasure with the President and the Congress.

In view of the foregoing, voters in November 2012 should carry the telephone number for the State Troopers in event something suspicious is noted at the voting station, and leaving there to use a public telephone or cell phone to alert the State Troopers.

A MAN AFTER MY
OWN HEART IN 2012

A friend in California sent me an article written by a Black author I had never heard of, MYCHAL S. MASSIE, with a list of his accomplishments on the last page. But I am getting ahead of myself. The caption on the front page read: Subject: Fwd: A Black's Perspective on the Obamas. Below that, a caption read "THE DAILY RANT". Below that in smaller letters, "Hard Hitting Conservative Commentary" with a copyright symbol after "THE DAILY RANT". The subject of the article read: "WHY I DO NOT LIKE THE OBAMAS" with a date below that: 23 February 2012. At the bottom of each page was the following: Thursday, April 05, 2012 AOL: Papa Brew. The foregoing are identifying characteristics of the article, but I don't dare quote from the article without Mr. Massie's approval and I don't know how to get it. I recommend that the reader attempt locating a copy because it is so worthwhile reading.

A list of Mr. Massie's voluminous credentials include the following: National Chairman of the conservative black think tank, Project 21—The National Leadership Network of Black Conservatives, and a member of its' parent think tank, the National Center for Public Policy Research. In his official capacity with this free market public policy think tank, he has spoken at the U.S. Capitol, participated in numerous press conferences on Capitol Hill and the National Press Club.

ABOUT THE AUTHOR

He was born on Capitol Hill in Washington, D.C. in 1926. After high school, he volunteered for the U.S. Navy in 1944 and was assigned to a Navy Reefer for supply runs from Pearl Harbor to Okinawa during the ongoing battle there. On one of the return trips, he was in a typhoon in the China Sea, and aboard the only ship in the convoy to survive.

Later, he was shipwrecked and assigned to the aircraft carrier U.S.S. Hancock. On departing, his commendation stated "The loss of this man's services to the U.S. Navy is to be regretted."

After the war, he worked for Public Accountants and attended night school. In 1947, he married a former Lady Marine who lived next door on Capitol Hill. In 1950, he was awarded a Bachelor of Science degree from Columbus University of Washington,

D.C., and later attended Georgetown University's School of Foreign Service.

He entered Federal service in 1956 at the National Security Agency, and later, the Department of Defense. In 1962, he transferred to the Federal Aviation Administration and was awarded a Presidential Citation in 1965 for saving millions of dollars in aircraft maintenance. In 1972, he was awarded the designation Certified Internal Auditor. He retired in 1985 and devoted most of his time to research.

Printed in the United States
by Booksurge, LLC

Printed in the United States
By Bookmasters